Apostle Marvin K.Omede

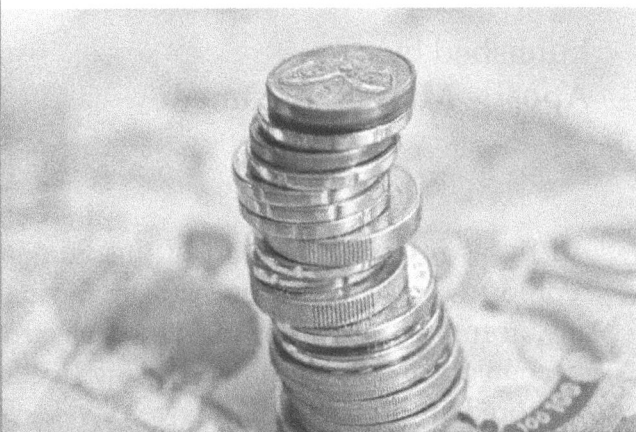

# KINGDOM WEALTH
## FOR BELIEVERS

A NEW APPROACH AT GETTING IT RIGHT
WITH MONEY AS A CHILD OF GOD.

# KINGDOM WEALTH FOR BELIEVERS

Apostle Marvin K. Omede
Copyright © 2019

$10.99
ISBN 978-1-7340657-0-1
51000>

9 781734 065701

Published by:
**Apostle Marvin K. Omede**

# Content

CHAPTER 1
The Secret of Divine Prosperity

CHAPTER 2
Operating The Covenant.

CHAPTER 3
Tithing And The Covenant

CHAPTER 4
My Encounter With The Holy Spirit On Giving..

CHAPTER 5
Income Distribution Chat

CHAPTER 6.
A Barrier To kingdom Financial Prosperity.

## PREFACE

*"The earth is the LORDs and the fullness thereof, the world and they that dwell therein"*
( Ps. 24:1.)

*"But thou shall remember the Lord thy God: for it is he that giveth thee power to get wealth, That he may establish his COVENANT which he Sware unto thy fathers, as it is this day"* (Deut. 8:18.)

*"And he brought us from thence, that he might bring us in, to give us the land which he sware unto our fathers.*
*And the LORD commanded us to do all these statues, to fear the Lord our God for our good always, that he might preserve us alive as it is this day.*
*And it shall be our righteousness, if we observe to do all these commandments, before the Lord our God, as he commanded us.*( Deut. 6:23-25)

*"The silver is mine and the gold is mine, saith the Lord of hosts"* (Hag. 2:8)

*Blessed be our father the Holy Spirit who has loved us, and given us all things that pertain unto life and godliness, through the knowledge of him that has called us to glory and virtues.*
( 1 Pet. 1:3).

Our God has blessed us from the above scriptures and the land here, (Deut. 6:23) represent your finance as well. Whatever your desires might be today, I have good news for you, God brought you out so that he bring you into his covenant WEALTH.

I don't know what you might have been struggling with that is affecting your flow of income as ordained by God the Holy Spirit, today you are coming out and entering gallantly into your COVENANT wealth of abundance and supernatural supply in Jesus name.
(John 10:10).

The kingdom finances and supply of wealth to mankind operate on certain Kingdom principles laid down by God almighty to keenly follow and obey, and the expectation of the righteous shall not be cut off.

And because our God cannot lie, and he is always faithful, he will do his own part of the covenant to enable you reap your harvest of wealth as a token for your obedience.

Welcome to supernatural supply of wealth.

The key principles that control divine wealth.

**SEED TIME AND HARVEST**

**GIVING AND RECEIVING**

**SOWING AND REAPING.**

The Holy Spirit said to my heart through a message and this simple lines hit my heart hard.

**" YOU DID NOT SOW,
FROM WHERE DID YOU WANT TO REAP?"**
Holy Spirit.

This was the simple lines that have all the secret to financial prosperity packed in itself…and I shouted **WHAT?**

And instantly all the information I have ever gathered, knowledge acquired during searches began to come together as a single piece, which resulted in my financial PEACE in family and Ministry.

This breakthrough also gave birth to income distribution CHAT in the kingdom and the book you have in your hand, as commanded by the Holy Spirit.

Please let me state here that when the Holy Spirit spoke and ask me the question about sowing. I was already a practicing tither; but the Holy Spirit always like when knowledge acquired is being shared to bless mankind and rescue others from financial mishap especially those in the body of Christ.

Perhaps this encounter came on March 30th 2018, so that I can put together all my financial resource materials, which the Holy Spirit has taught me both through books and others, by revelation to build my faith in obedience towards this important spiritual exercise called TITHING.

More details in later chapters regarding my personal encounter with God the Holy Spirit.
God is set to bless you and reward you abundantly as you obey these principles.

*"If ye be willing and obedient, ye shall eat the good of the land "* (Isa:1v19)

# THE COMMANDMENT.

*"You Write What You Know
And Put The Formula in There For Them"*
The Holy Spirit. July 7th, 2018.

# CHAPTER 1

# THE SECRET OF
# DIVINE PROSPERITY.

All glory to the Holy Ghost, it is one thing to teach secret, it is another thing for God to reveal the secret to you, as it applies to your position so that you can understand and use this truth of supernatural supplies from the scriptures to your advantage in building his church.

*"The secret things belong unto the Lord our God; but those things which are revealed belong unto us and our children forever, that we may do all the words of this law"* Deut. 29:29.

You can only share facts from your own personal experience with God through practical proof before it can render help and impact others who hear you.

These are my own lines of words as inspired by the Holy Spirit the greatest teacher, who has taught me and guided me to understand the knowledge of Kingdom prosperity at the level that I am now in ministry.

The Holy Spirit has also supplied the motivation and grace to share this knowledge as you will read in the story below.

Therefore, as you read, I encourage you to open up your heart and allow the Holy Spirit to open your eyes and understanding **(Luke 24:31, 45)**, to see His power in finance and abundant wealth he has provided for the church.

Why did I mention **"to see"**, until you see it you cannot hold it, **until you understand it,** you cannot use it.

A lot of us were in church for a long time, listening to the stories of kingdom prosperity and covenant wealth but no revelation. So your personal revelation from the Holy Spirit is to see and understand how it works.

As you will read in later chapters, I have been a student of kingdom prosperity for a long time, but there was no revelation so there was NO IMPACT upon my life and ministry. I pray that today, your eyes of understanding will be enlighten in Jesus name, Amen.

The last and major ENCOUNTER that lifted the veil off my eyes happened on March 10$^{th}$, 2018. I have been living the life of a tither before this time, but the good thing about this awesome encounter through the word of God was, it brought together all the revelations and other encounters I have had with the Holy Spirit, regarding finance in the body of Christ and made them a perfect whole. That is giving me full understanding of what I needed to know, letting me know why what I was practicing was working.

Sometimes, you may be practicing something as a believer, but you may not have a full revelation behind it, to the extent of being a blessing to others. I want to believe that it was that singular revelation I got on March 30$^{th}$ that gave birth to further encounter that resulted to the book you have in your hand now.

I have come to realize that in life, *whatever you don't understand you cannot use.*

This must be the reason why in Luke 24:45 **Jesus opened up the disciples understanding.**

*"Then opened he their understanding that they might understand the scriptures."* Luke: 24v45
This was what I heard that beautiful evening that changed all my thinking and rearranged all my knowledge about covenant wealth, as I was listening to a message of my spiritual father in the Lord, Bishop David Oyedepo, on the secret of finance, I heard him say boldly,
**" YOU DID NOT SOW, FROM WHERE DO YOU WANT TO REAP"** The Holy Spirit
But this statement sounded so loud and hit my heart and all my thinking cells became reactivated. The best way to describe it, the Holy Spirit, re-echoed it for me to hear and it hit me so hard that I was looking for where to quickly take down note of what I just heard. So I quickly wrote down the date and time of this uncommon encounter from the Holy Spirit. Mind you, this wasn't the first time I am hearing this statement, in September 2016, the Holy Spirit said to me directly while in a Church Service under the same anointing,

*"Have you ever seen anyone sowing and frowning their face"*

No I answered, he said **WHY?"** The Holy Spirit.

Details about this September encounter in 2016 will be in further chapters where I shared all my personal encounters with the Holy Spirit that brought me and my Ministry to this point. Please don't get me wrong, we are not where we want to be yet, or neither have we arrived where the Holy Spirit is taking me or the Ministry to, but as my custom is, in Christ Jesus by the Power of the Holy Ghost, I have always celebrated, every instruction and COMMAND from my loving Father the Holy Spirit, who has been leading me and still lead me to this day.

I write down in my prophetic note, every little thing he tells me, there was a time he asked me in 2016, "IS IT EVERYTHING YOU WRITE"
I write because I value them. The Holy Spirit does not talk casually, he doesn't say what he doesn't intend to do. To some believers, you may have the working knowledge of kingdom finance, but to others it is still a mystery, that is the purpose for this book as commanded by the Holy Spirit, to shield light into those mysterious areas in a nut shell.

In another glory encounter on July 17$^{th}$ 2018, I

heard the Holy Spirit said to me in clear words:
**"YOU WRITE WHAT YOU KNOW AND PUT THE FORMULA IN THERE FOR THEM"**
The Holy Spirit.

The complete details of this encounter will be in the chapter where I shared other revelations. This is to let you know that, by grace this little book was commanded, that is the only reason why it will have impact. I pray that the virtues of the Holy Spirit accompanying this material will liberate and open up the understanding of believers, as it regards finance in the kingdom.
And I pray the Holy Spirit visit you in his own way in Jesus name. Amen

**Financial Mentors in Kingdom Finance.**
I have said a few things about my humble self, because I have  never been qualified but only operating on grace, to know those men and women that God the Holy Spirit has placed on my path in life to keenly follow them, before meeting them in person., if ever I will meet some of them.

Bishop David Oyedepo, is one man I have admired and wondered at how he got to where he is today in life and Ministry commanding enormous wealth, coupled with all that he says regarding how

God has been faithful to bless financially in the Kingdom. While others have no single clue, how these things works.

This baffled me, and I like to ask questions, I began to search to know for myself how this thing works as a believer.

And I know that the best way to learn is to learn by example, I have read the book he read that gave him his breakthrough by the help of God, (**God's Will is Prosperity**- *Gloria Copeland).*

I have been following him closely trying to learn the secrets of Covenant Wealth that God revealed to him in an encounter he gladly teaches, but I have come to realize, t**hat until you follow heartily (Col. 3:23-24), one may not see what the other saw,** or *until the Holy Spirit opens your eyes* **(Luke 24:31)** *and understanding.*

(Luke 24:45) this revelation may remain a mystery. I pray by the power of the Holy Ghost, your eyes shall be open to see and receive fresh revelations from this book in Jesus mighty name. Amen. Even if it's just a line of words, you shall grasp your own word (Isa. 9:8) in Jesus name, Amen.

*"Therefore with Joy, shall you draw water out of the wells of salvation."* ( Isa. 12:3).

I have followed with Joy, for over a decade in trying to learn the secret of divine prosperity, and how it runs in life and ministry. The secret of divine prosperity remain concealed to so many even believers, because it is the pleasure of the Lord to conceal it and it is our duty to search it out.

It is in the aspect of searching that a lot of believers are missing it.

But I will advice that whenever a truth is revealed in the body of Christ, we believers should embrace and run with it.

**(Hab:2v1-3).**

Glory to God who has made the secret of kingdom wealth revealed to one of his servant in our days, otherwise, a lot of believers would still be praying, fasting and casting for Finance in the body of Christ. Because what the Lord says to one , he says to all: it is wisdom to apply these principles to be blessed.

This is core of the revelation on Covenant Wealth as God showed his servant Bishop David Oyedepo. One may say , why should I believe him? Well, I believed because as one privileged to hear from God directly, the Holy Spirit gave me a separate revelation confirming Bishop David Oyedepo has one  of those that has the keys to Covenant wealth in our days. This is why I have to patiently stay calm and learn.

This is the message he was given from God when he went searching,
.May 22<sup>nd</sup> 1982.
**"My prosperity plan is a COVENANT and not a PROMISE,** *which has no respect for **PRAYER** and **FASTING***, *until your part is played I    am not committed* '

Through this revelation , a lot of believers and ministers alike have dived into sudden supernatural wealth by committing to the obedience of this principle of TITHING. YES , YOUR PART THERE IN THE COMMAND, IS YOUR TITHE.
When you pay your tithe as a believer, you have given God the opportunity to bless you supernaturally, following, (Mal. 3v10-11.)

**A COVENANT.**

**What Is a covenant?**

A covenant is an agreement between two people, which is sealed with an oath.
*" My covenant will I not break, nor alter the thing*

*that is gone out of my lips."* (Psa: 89v34).

This is God Almighty sending his word of assurance to you and I, that as far you go along to obey my covenant of tithing, I will stand on my word because I cannot lie, and I cannot break my covenant.
*"while the earth remaineth seed time and harvest....shall not cease"*
(Gen:8v20-22).

This became a law unto Abraham, our father of faith. And it simply stand for until you sow a seed, an harvest will not be in view. Our harvest largely depend on what we have sown. When you have not sown a seed, do not expect an harvest.
Remember I said that what he says to one, he says to all **(Mark:13v37).** If only we can stay with the Holy Spirit and study the dept of this revelation and go further to apply this knowledge, no child of God will have to under go financial stress in the kingdom. The secret to covenant prosperity has been revealed unto us **(Deut:29v29)** who is ready to believe and accept the conditions, and go further to apply the covenant requirements of **"SEED TIME AND HARVEST"** as revealed to God servant Bishop David Oyedepo in this great encounter.

But *"who has believed our report, and to whom is the arm of the Lord revealed"* (Isa:53v1).

I pray that the Holy Spirit will by his power open the eyes of your understanding as you read, and that every secret of divine prosperity shall rest on your bosom in Jesus name. Amen.

This my most favourite part of this encounter, this great man of God had, he asked the Lord, **"what assurance do I have, that when I SOW MY SEED, it will always lead to my HARVEST, how do I know, that this COVENANT will always be there?**

What should I build my confidence upon, even though I already know you cannot lie?" ( Paraphrased, according to my understanding to enable you grasp its dept).

The good Lord now replied from Jere:33v20-21. *"Thus saith the Lord, if ye can break my COVENANT of the DAY, and my COVENANT of the NIGHT, and that there should not be day and night in their season. Then will my COVENANT be broken with David my servant..."*

This I believed and received, all I have been working on personally before now is to ensure I apply it adequately and diligently, so that the profiting may appear unto all. As many that received him (his word) **(John:1v1) to them gave he POWER,** (John:1v12). *"But thou shall remember the Lord thy God, for it is he that giveth thee POWER to get wealth"*

May you receive that power today in Jesus name. Amen.

You and I just have to trust the Holy Spirit on this, to fulfill his part, of the covenant when we have done our part by sowing. Because we serve a God who can neither lie or fail, it is impossible for him to lie. Even when we are not faithful, he will always be faithful to keep his promise, but **TITHING IS NOT A "BIBLICAL PROMISE", it is a COVENANT.**

Let me surprise you with this, in this covenant of tithing, God is waiting for you and I to just obey and play our part, his part of the deal is settled in heaven. You just obey and see his windows of heaven open abundantly to you and your household; that you won't have enough store to keep the OUTPOURING OF HIS BLESSINGS. That's what the word of God says, and I believe it can happen for you. **(Mal:3v10).**

The secret has just been placed in your hands, read further and see what the Lord revealed to me regarding the wealth of his kingdom for the church

# CHAPTER 2

# OPERATIONS OF
# THE COVENANT

We have established, that the prosperity plan of God is operated by a covenant and not based on promise. But how is the covenant operated, how do I apply it? Through seed time and harvest.

*'While the earth remaineth seed time and harvest , and cold and heat, and summer and winter, and day and night shall not cease."* Gen:8v22

My brethren, the same principle that works for seed time and harvest as regarding practicalising the covenant, also work for the law of sowing and reaping.

*" Be not deceived, God is not mocked, for whatsoever a man soweth, that shall he also reap"* Gal:6v7

That is from the scripture above, you shall reap what you sow, my light (revelation) which the Holy Spirit used to give me breakthrough and peace in kingdom finance came from this scripture. Which will be explained in later chapter. The above system of financial operations, in the kingdom also cover **"Giving and Receiving"**.

It is amazing, how this three separate but similar scripture connects to make a whole. **The only way up in the kingdom of God, financially is by giving.** *With the same measure you give, the same shall be given back to you.,*

*" Give and it shall be given unto you, good measure, Pressed down, and shaken together, shall men give unto your bosom, for with the same measure that ye mete , with it shall be measured to you.* **Luk:6v38.**

From the above revelation, if we say the divine law of prosperity is based on **the covenant of seed time and harvest, sowing and reaping, giving and receiving.**

What assurance do I have from scriptures to operate this covenant of prosperity.

What should I build my confidence upon.?

This is the answer, God cannot break is covenant,

he also said that if he obey this principle of tithing. This is another reason to build your faith.

*" Thus saith, the Lord, if you can break my covenant of the day, and my covenant of the night, and that there should not be day and night in their season, then may also my covenant with David my servant, that he not have a son to reign upon his throne, and the levites  that ministers unto me.* (Jere:33v20-21).

This means, that as long as you wake up to see, the sun and moon in place, the day and the night in place, which are also my covenant, this means that my covenant of seed time and harvest is still in place. Whenever you sow, you will reap an harvest. Whenever you give your tithe and offering you must be blessed in return.

That shall be your testimony in Jesus name. Amen.

My beloved, I try to see the reason why this concept of financial prosperity in the kingdom, keep eluding so many people; to some people, it seems so simple that tithing can make you rich in the kingdom. And others think that what is the relationship between my giving and my wealth as a child of God?

I will explain this further in later chapter, but as a way of setting a foundation to break that misconception which is robbing a lot of Christians of their covenant right.

By his mercies, the Holy Spirit, seeing my heart desire and state of mind, that I needed to get this concept right to enable me get top the next level of my kingdom wealth, as I was listening to this preacher of Prosperity in the Christian faith.

## " YOU DID NOT SOW, FROM WHERE DO YOU WANT TO REAP"

I want to believe that this revelation came to me, simply because I am a teacher, so I could pass the knowledge across to others. And explained to those innocent believers who sincerely want to obey this commandment, but could not simply relate how giving, sowing or tithing could to their being financially wealthy in the kingdom of God.

TITHING obeys the natural law of giving and receiving as well, *just like you cannot start your car, without having gasoline in the tank, the car won't respond to the command of the engine,* is that simple. That is how it is, **your tithe fuels your financial FAVOUR from God.** That is why I will even rebuke the devourer for your sake, why? Because he has blessed you from your tithing.

This is one thing I learn also about importance of tithe and offering, ( giving).

**IT DOES NOT ONLY AFFECT YOUR FINANCE AND LIFT YOU UP, IT WORKS ON AND WITH YOUR ENTIRE LIFE AND LIFESTYLE!**

Have you seen a giver recently, they are always cheerful and full of joy, which comes as a result of their giving nature. And they are blessed in return.

And as believers we shouldn't doubt the aspect of the Holy Spirit blessing us, when we have done our part. He said in Malachi, **"PROVE ME NOW"**, meaning you do your part of this my covenant and see what happens. God was just confidently, and boldly declaring in all his authority, **DARE ME, if I won't bless you beyond your ability to achieve. Beyond, what your present strength, can produce,** that is what we call GODS BLESSINGS!

**BLESSINGS FROM TITHING**

And this is another area, where a lot of people miss it about tithing, when you have given your tithe, God the Holy Spirit, in his infinite wisdom, can decide to bless you in other ways other than money. These blessings can come in the form of divine ideas for prosperity in business, sudden opening of new chapters in your chosen area of field or career. He can release unto you and your family, divine health, that none shall be feeble or sick in your household, as a result of your tithing. And his protection from your going out daily to work and coming back in, meeting everyone in peace. That can be as a result of your tithing, REBUKING the devourer from laying filthy hand on any member of your family. So my beloved, the REWARD, of tithing is not only seen in our finances, but tied to our entire life as a believer. Take a look at this,

*" And ye shall serve the LORD your God, and he shall BLESS thy Bread and thy water, and I will take sickness away from the midst of thee.*
*There shall nothing cast their young, nor be barren in the land,*
*The number of days I will fulfil.* (Exodus:23v25-26)

As you can see, the whole blessings package, as explained above is all touched here in this scripture, to the extent of fulfilling your own days with longevity.

**Only God can guarantee that**. So let no unbelief steal your blessings.

Brethren this is what we know, that is why we don't doubt it, and joyfully and hopefully pays our tithe **like the sincere and diligent farmer,** *who sows his seed and expects his harvest, knowing that nature does not cheat in bringing her returns for sowing seed.* ( **Seed time and harvest remaineth**) Gen:8v22.

Let us take for instance, before now, like I was

during training, even as a Christian, it was difficult for me to understand. Sometimes, I want to pay, but my faith and conviction wasn't strong enough, especially when you don't even have so much money to spare. This I understand, maybe the Holy Spirit allowed me pass through that road, for your sake. So that some day, you can read this short story and comprehend in full areas that you may have been missing it.

**IF WE DON'T GIVE, WE WLL NOT RECEIVE FROM THE BLESSER.**
**AND THE BLESSER IS GOD, BECAUSE WE ARE THE BLESSED.**

*For it is written …*Proverb:10v22

*"The blessing of the LORD, it maketh rich, and it addeth no sorrow with it."*
This is what I want us to understand, it is the HOLY SPIRIT, that blesses.  Let us not think like unbelievers, thinking that it is our labour or effort that will make us rich.

For *"The earth is the LORD, and the fullness thereof; the world and they that dwell therein. For he hath founded it upon the seas and established upon the floods"* (Psalm:24v1-2).

My dear brethren in Christ Jesus, let the world be talking, and doubt tithing, but you just obey. Even as you read the I pray that the grace to believe, be released unto you in Jesus name. I had this personal encounter with the Holy Spirit and I am sharing it with you for your own lifting, my life is a TESTIMONY till date.

And I desire you have the faith to be like in **Hebrew 4v2;** the same message that was given to us was also given to them, but they did not believe, because they did not miss what they heard with faith ( paraphrased). This scripture just proved that there is a blessing attached to BELIEVING.

*" For unto us was the gospel preached, as well as unto them; But the WORD preached did not profit them, not being mixed FAITH, in them that heard it."* Heb:4v2

And when you have obeyed this word and give cheerfully according to your level per time, the Bible says;
*" All nations shall call you blessed. For ye shall be a delightsome land, saith the LORD of host"*(Malac:3v12).

This shall become your own testimony in Jesus name. The Holy Spirit will give you a new song. I decree and I pray that if you have been struggling before now, not being able to account for your finances and you are working; the hand of the Holy Spirit, the protector will take care of your finances from henceforth, and rebuke every devourer in Jesus name. Amen.

Even the devourer of unbelief shall be visited hastily and destroyed in your life in Jesus name. Amen. You are FREE to prosper.

# CHAPTER 3

## TITHING, DIVINE PROSPERITY AND THE COVENANT.

### WHAT IS TITHING?

Tithing is a supernatural covenant initiated by God, to bless believers.

*" But thou shall remember the Lord thy God ,For it is he that giveth thee POWER to get wealth"*
( Deut:8v18)
Tithing is a spiritual transaction between you and God based on covenant practice that will earned you profiting if willingly obeyed.

*" if ye be willing and obedient, ye shall eat  the good of the land"* (Isa:1v19)

Tithing is an orchestrated financial design put together by God to divinely solve the financial challenge of any believer who choose to obey this commandment.

Tithing is giving ten percent of all your increase to God which in turn blesses you supernaturally in your most important areas of need which may not be finance in some return. ( The return for your tithing can come in form of divine health, unspeakable joy, Peace beyond understanding and through divine ideas in business and careers)

Tithing is a source of supernatural wealth, which open doors to abundant riches, based on God's covenant of seed time and harvest.

*"Bring ye all the tithe into the store house, That there may be meat in my house, and prove me now, herewith saith the Lord, of host if I will not open you the windows of heaven and pour you out a blessing that there shall not be room enough to receive it"* Mal:3v10

A man of God said and I quote, **"we haven't really given until we have paid our tithe"**. And I completely agree with him.
There is no other **"given"** in the Bible that was so

much **stressed,** and with **emphasis,** as to the extent of having a reward of abundance and even rebuking the devourer for your sake when you give in obedience.

What happens to the man that refuse to give his tithe in obedience, simply put, the man who disobeys will have to deal with the devourer himself.

But remember, *except the Lord build a house, they labour in vain that build it, except the Lord keep the city, the watchman waketh but in vain"* (Ps:127v1.) My advice is, let the Holy Spirit build your house and your finance, I bet you, you did be happy you did. Give Him a chance, by learning the secret of finance in the kingdom and I promise you, it will be worth it.

If the Lord says he is going to rebuke the devourer when you pay your tithe, from destroying your fruits (your finance, health, job or whatever makes you happy)

What happens to your income when you do not pay your tithe, the exact opposite happens.

Please let me state here that, in my understanding , the Lord will not directly destroy what you have, but when he takes away his covering, his protection, over you, the enemy comes in to do their evil work which is in **(John:10v10.)**

Be wise and get into his covering, by sowing 10% of your increase to the church of God where you are being blessed and feed spiritually.

Sometimes ago, a friend challenged me, show me where Jesus said we should pay our tithe in the new testament, that tithing is an old doctrine, and went away with the old commandment in the old testament; within few days of his asking, the Holy Spirit led me to Heb:7v5.

*"And verily, they that are of the sons of Levi, who receive the office of the priesthood, have a commandment to take tithes of the people according to the law, that is of their brethren, though they came out of the Loins of Abraham"*

So we are to pay tithe, it is a commandment to pay tithe to the priest who oversee your spiritual life, this is biblical and pleases God.

**WHO RECEIVES THE TITHE IN HEAVEN?**

I can say with assurance and revelation, that **Jesus Christ** collects the tithes in heaven and distributes the blessings according.

" Few years ago, by revelation the Holy Spirit revealed to me, **that all tithes, paid here on earth** are collected in a purse in  heaven or a closed box containing spiritual money with your name on it. **The only way that box will be remembered and opened for financial transaction is when your tithes goes up to Jesus in heaven and on arrival, the box containing your spiritual money is then opened, and your blessings sent down according to your percentage increase here on earth"** so when you don't pay your tithe, you have instructed heaven to please keep your box closed that you are satisfied here on earth, that you need nothing.

(Mind you, the return from your tithing may not come in the form of money, sometimes the Holy Spirit answers our Prayers in the areas of our lives were we need urgent attention, it may come in the form of divine health, Peace in the family, success at work or academic pursuit, getting a marriage partner, all these are avenues of payback for your tithe.) Which most of us ignore and expect physical cash, in return for tithing always and make us ungrateful to the ever faithful God.

I can clearly remember an encounter the blessed man of God, Kenneth Hagin had with the Holy Spirit, in a situation where a brother, a young evangelist who was just starting out in Ministry, needed money, the Lord told Kenneth Hagin to give this person $10, which was much money to

Kenneth Hagin to give away at that time, there was a slight argument about whether to give it or not, but finally he obeyed and gave it.

The second time was for a stranded preacher, I think this was $12.50.

While the man was preaching the Holy Spirit told Kenneth Hagin " I want you to give him $12.50 out of your pocket" that money seems small now, but it was more than a week salary for Kenneth Hagin then, he struggled but also at the end gave out the money to bless the man of God as instructed by the Holy Spirit.

Now, how was Kenneth Hagin rewarded, for his obedience in giving, ( note; this is not tithing…just giving).

The LORD USED HIM TO RAISE SOMEONE FROM A DEATHBED. AWESOME!

*"if you hadn't obeyed me on that, I couldn't have used you here"* **the Lord said.**

You see my brethren, only the Holy Spirit, has the sole right to decide how to bless you in return for your Tithe, offerings and giving, I think our role is to humbly obey his command and trust him that cannot lie, but even give to us most times, things that money cannot buy, but what only God can do. The level of divine health most of us enjoy, not to taste drugs with your mouth or for more than three years you won't know what is called sickness or disease; money can't buy that it can only be a blessing from God the Holy Spirit.

All glory to his name. Amen.

Therefore, Jesus is the one who takes the tithe in heaven, let us pay it with honour. *'"And here men that die, receive tithe, but there he receiveth them (where? Heaven) of whom it is witnessed that he liveth.* (Heb:7v8).

In one of past studies, Jesus appeared to Oral Roberts in that revelation, and said to him. *"Tell your member in church and partners to pay their tithe. If not I won't be able to bless them if they don't give.* They should obey me first by paying their tithe. Which is similar in revelation to what the Holy Ghost revealed to me on the **"heavenly pulse"** that can only be remembered and opened until your tithe goes up to God. All glory to the Holy Ghost.

**DIVINE PROSPERITY AND THE COVENANT.**

I thank God the Holy Spirit, that he made divine prosperity a **covenant** and not a **promise**. Meaning when we pay our tithe, which is the first in the covenant of giving, also we give to the Church as donation, we give to the poor, we pay our offering in Chruch, all these connect us to a spiritual transaction with the Holy Spirit who is always faithful to his word. You must surely have your reward ready when you have obeyed.

*"if ye be willing and obedient ye shall eat the good of the Land."* Isa:1v19.

So with the understanding of tithing being a covenant between me and God, my giving gives me personal peace. Therefore I don't really care, how others feel or react about the money given or received, because it is a spiritual exercise, it takes those that believes to obey and receive. Our focus should rather be on Jesus Christ, who made the covenant, and receives the tithe to bless us according to our giving.

**Jesus cannot fail or make mistakes, therefore our finances are secured with him, in safe hands and I must get back my reward for giving, because he is faithful.**

Is that not interesting? what greater assurance do we need when we are dealing directly with God Almighty.

Do you now know why most Christians are not blessed financially in the body of Christ? No matter how they go to Church, praise God or read the Bible.

It is simply, *because the law that govern financial*

*blessings in the kingdom of God is a Covenant that must be first obeyed,* and not debated, as many do.Until this covenant is obeyed as stated in scripture by giving, there is no REWARD in view.

Just as the Holy Spirit revealed this to his servant Bishop David Oyedepo, *"this part of my blessing;* **DOES NOT ANSWER TO PRAYER AND FASTING"**

Therefore, Christians should not confuse this concept of kingdom prosperity or financial matters in the kingdom with prayer and fasting, or with church attendance, this ones have their place differently.

Only tithing answers to our finances as designed by our maker, God Almighty.

And I want to humbly state here that, please do not feel intimidated, or ashamed of yourself, it doesn't MATTER, where you find yourself in this ladder of spiritual exercise (tithing). In most cases, it is the Holy Spirit himself that trains us to become obedient and diligent tithers as believers. It is not because we are smarter or know it all. So this book, is not to discourage you or show you your weakness, in the area of giving or tithing, but to make you see, by the anointing of the Holy Ghost, **1 John:2v27),** that this may be what is remaining to be done to lift you into your next level of abundant wealth in Christ Jesus by faith.

My brethren, nobody will dare to criticize you, because we all came to where we are today by grace. Even the master givers (tithers) in the body of Christ, were once babies in giving, some doubting it just as you did in the past. That is why if you hear some of their testimony, you will see that the Holy Spirit have to train them to become givers, in their early days of struggling with this exercise.

For example, he may ask some to give their most precious possession then like the only car in the family, a lot of our great preachers today, did out of fear, trembling and by faith in God obeyed and today, the reward is still speaking for them. Others where tried to give up their salaries, (6 months or more), some it was half of their gratuity ( all that remains for them to live on for the rest of their life), what is the Holy Spirit doing with this exercise, by asking you to give up some of your most cherished and precious possession? He is graciously introducing us into the school of TITHING. So it is not what you memorize, it is what becomes a part of you. If you are a GIVER, you are a giver!

The point I am making here is, be excited, at any level that you are, because, even with what you are reading now, the Holy Spirit has began the process of training you to become a champion in the ministry of giving. Until you too will begin to share your experience with others later.

My own case, was a blessed one. I began my Christian journey by doubting a lot of things in the body of Christ. Maybe it was because of my scientific  background, or that I am naturally curious. With me, then, you have to explain everything black and white. That is I want to see, how it all happen. But I never knew that Gods way are not like that, and that a lot of things in the body of Christ, cannot literally be explained like I demanded then. That is why the Bible, says in Luke: 1v45;

*" And blessed is she that believed, for there shall be a performance of those things that was told her from the Lord"*

So I was trained by the Holy Spirit, and grew up to believe what God says, and stop analyzing the scripture with my physical eyes and canal knowledge. **(Deut:29v29)**. Spirituality is a mystery, that is why you and I need the help of the Holy Spirit to teach us always, areas we may be lacking like this issue of tithing.

So I got to where I am today by training, and you may have read the diverse revelation and divine encounters as a result of training. Humorously, the Holy Spirit is so kind, in my case, and my personal experience, during my early days. Immediately I am paid, and I made the decision to pay my tithe out of that money, before separating it and making the actual payment, a new business will be waiting for me inline. I will ask myself, but LORD, I have not paid my tithe yet?

I knew when the kind gesture continued that it was the Holy Spirit way of encouraging me that this exercise is REAL. And that he alone truly blesses those that give. So I don't know what your training will look like, but please open your heart and be prepared to learn.

A lot of believers are still struggling and can't lay a hold of the reason why?

From my knowledge, if it is finances, please check your giving life, beginning from tithing. Every great man today, who is doing well financially in the body of Christ, and is a tither, has their story and their time of training. From what you read above, you saw the little amount the Holy Spirit asked Kenneth Hagin to give? Did you see where the blessing of the money came back to him? Was the reward in monetary term, NO! He blessed him another way, but Kenneth Hagin who has obeyed financially won't lack money coupled with extra blessing and anointing for healing.( The Holy Spirit used him to heal a man from a deathbed, the man was dying.) is that not a miracle. Some of us are expecting a blessing here, and in this area, we are refusing to obey God, who knows what our next blessing is tied to.

May the Holy Spirit grant us understand. For it is written:

*"... ... having done  ALL, TO STAND!*
*STAND  THEREFORE,  Having  your  loins  girth about with truth, And having on the breast plate of righteousness.* (Eph:6v13-14)

The Holy Spirit expect you  to take a stand and begin to build on the foundation of giving so that your next chapter shall be full of the stories and testimonies of abundance in Jesus name. Amen. **ONLY BELIEVE!  SEE YOU AT THE VERY TOP.**

**WHAT YOU MUST DO TO BE BLESSED.**

You and I have a role to play in the Covenant chain in order for us to be blessed. God cannot break his covenant for our lack of understanding, or lack of the will  to obey.

Most believers in church today, want to get blessed

first before they will obey or some others want to be blessed without sowing a seed.

I can imagine the Holy Spirit asking, **my son, my daughter, what do you want me to bless you with, where is your seed.**

Naturally, from the real world, you will agree with me that as a farmer, *you cannot reap a crop without sowing a seed.* **Until you put a seed into the ground**, *nothing will come out for harvest,* so my beloved , it is exact same way for our finance. **What you sow, you are qualify to reap in harvest.**

My brethren, as you read further, you will see how the Sweet Holy Spirit has led me, teaching me along side in this journey for you to be blessed.

Who knows it may have been for your sake, that I have to go through this route, for you to have this book in your hand and read about my experience that joined in lifting me up as an apostle of God by grace.

Today I thank God I obeyed his instructions and teachings as I followed him in faith during my training process. You too must take a stand and do something about your financial life, giving in to spiritual diligence.

You will not missed your reward in Jesus name. Amen.

# CHAPTER 4

## MY ENCOUNTERS WITH THE HOLY SPIRIT ON GIVING

I came to the understanding that after studies and guidance by the Holy Spirit that, *"what they give you never enriches you, rather it is what you give that makes you rich"* **what a kingdom principle.**

A lot of us have the mentality, that the more we receive, the more we are blessed.

Remember the scripture *says "Give and it shall be given unto you...* Luk:6v38.

And well said, and emphasized more by Jesus in **Acts:20v35.**

*"I have showed you all things, how that so laboring ye ought to the weak,* **and remember the words of the Lord Jesus how he said**
*"it is more blessed to give than to receive"*

That is a shift of mindset, the financial law in the kingdom does not operate the order way round. **You GIVE first, you SOW first, before REAPING, and you PLANT a seed first before harvest.**
And we have stated earlier that breakthrough into financial abundance begins with you tithing.

## WHAT IS TITHING?
Tithing is releasing one tenth or ten percent of all your increase to God. It is a spiritual transaction between you and God who commanded it, and ensures the release of his blessings upon everyone who obeys.

*" And all the tithe of the land, whether of the seed of the Land, or of the fruit of the tree, is the Lord, it is holy unto the Lord"* Lev:27v30.

Tithing is the secret key to financial stability and freedom in the kingdom. So Many believers are searching for how it operates. Especially Gods servants ( Pastors who may be having challenges in the area of their ministry).
Until we get it right with God, we keep searching.
It all lies in the obedience of his commandment for

tithing.

*" And it shall come to pass, if thou shall hearken diligently Unto the voice of the Lord, thy God to observe and to do all His commandment, which I command thee this day, that the Lord thy God will set thee on high, above all nations of the earth. And all this blessing shall come on thee, and overtake thee, if thou hearken unto the voice of the LORD thy God"* ( Deut:28v1-2)

Did you see where He said all these blessings shall come on thee, just for the obedience of his commandment. Brethren, I chose to obey than struggle in ignorance.

## MY JOURNEY WITH THE HOLY SPIRIT IN TITHING.

On the 19th of July, 2015, where the message of tithing and financial prosperity was being taught. Half way into the service, I heard the Holy Spirit screamed loudly into my outer ear, from Mal:3v10 " **PROVE ME NOW**".

Meaning you obey my command, begin your tithing consistently and prove me.

What was happening that the Holy Ghost have to scream at me, to be steadfast.

I was paying my tithe then, but I wasn't consistent; maybe because I haven't gotten the dept of revelation, or understanding that I have now about tithing.

So I was struggling with it, even though God desired to bless me more, I was personally holding Him back because of my attitude and inconsistency. I can't forget that experience I heard Him clearly.

So when people doubt the commandment and validity of tithing as a kingdom source of wealth, I say simply, you need to hear from God. I have heard and I have a personal experience.

*"If ye be willing and obedient, ye shall*
*Eat the fruit of the land"*
( Isa:1v19.)

Recently, I found myself asking the reverse of Gods commandment; this is where most people don't like how we relate with God. I thought about it, **" what if you refuse to be willing and obedient, what will you eat?**

You are in the best place to answer for yourself,

may the Holy Spirit grants you understanding.
(Luk:24v45).

## THE NIGHT VISION.

That was not all, the Holy Spirit taught me, also about giving. September 4th 2016, before I went to bed to sleep. I ask the Holy Spirit, show me what I need to know about? Then I slept, in a night vision (I had a dream). I couldn't remember the dream fully, so I went back to sleep consciously to find out what the Lord has shown me in the night vision (dream). Because I was sure I had an encounter that I shouldn't let slip.

The second time I slept, I heard him said to me clearly, " Any mark place by the enemy, counter them in the name of Jesus, and he gave me a scripture to cover my entire vision and revelation of that dream. And also to confirm what I need to be doing, from the questions I asked before I slept. **The scripture is (Isa:32v8).**

I jumped off the bed to search for it and it reads.

*"But the liberal deviseth liberal things, And by liberal things shall he stand."*Isa:32v8.

When I read, I perceived in my spirit that I should start giving and giving more.
That is making giving an habit, so that He can bless

me.

This was the encounter I had that led me into giving willingly and stresslessly.

I hope this will be a blessing to someone, whose heart is desiring to get it right with God. **No matter the level, you are in tithing and in giving do not condemn yourself.**(Rom:8v1). *Tithing and giving are both spiritual exercise.* You may see it ordinary, it is not and never will be, it is a spiritual activity that connects you with God and the spirit realm.

How come sometimes, God the Holy Spirit himself will command, and tell you in some cases specifically how to give for a project, or to someone for him to bless you in return.

I am sharing my story, And I know that I am not the only one that came through this path as we speak, so many Christians and Pastors have not seen this secret and find this key to kingdom wealth. May the Lord open your eyes to see  and ear to hear in the name of Jesus. As for you, as a prophet of God, I curse every veil covering your access to Kingdom truth in financial prosperity so that you  too can be free in Jesus name.

This time you will see the light as you approach this book in simplicity. (Psalm:119v130). Remember there is connecting scriptures to the revelation from **(Isaiah:32v8).**

*"But the liberal deviseth liberal things, And by liberal things shall he stand."*

**"The liberal soul shall be made fat, and he that watereth, shall be watered also himself"** (Prov:11v25).

My beloved, the law cannot change because of us, it has been established before we were born.**"He that watereth, the same shall be watered"**. Did you see that you have to water first....

The Liberal soul shall be fat. You must be liberal first, before your fatness comes in financial resources, and ideas, and divine health, peace, promotion and all round rest.

*"And the Lord gave them rest round about".*

I release upon you today, the grace to obey willingly.**(Isaiah:11v19).**

So that you too can eat the good of the land. There is good in that land you are, it is God that connected you, only him can release it for you to access it.

At least by now, you have an understanding of what to do.

**It is seed time before harvest time.** Shortly, I will show you a simple principle to spread your income to enable you tithe, and give easily without stress.

"I CALL IT THE GIVING FORMULA". Where no

matter what you earn you will be able to give someone a little. It is all about understanding how the principle works.

Most times we have the mentality that I don't have energy as I don't earn enough, how can I give. And also let me state here that giving in the kingdom is in level.

Give according to your capacity, *"For God loveth a Cheerful giver"* (2$^{nd}$ Cor:9v7).

**THE FARMERS ILLUSTRATION.**

The training with the Holy Spirit continues on tithing and giving.

The third encounter was on September 2016. One may wonder why several revelation, just because of simple tithe, offering and giving.

Maybe it is because, one day I will have to share the knowledge and process he took me through to get my key to financial freedom in the kingdom.

I am not here to boast, I have always been a learner and still is, this is exactly how I got here today. Financially free, strong and sound on tithing and giving principles. The Bible says that *you shall know the truth and the truth shall set you free.* Won't you want to be free? It is only revealed answers that can set one free in dealing with kingdom secrets. I pray for you, that through this, you will access your freedom in Jesus name.

September 2016, I was in a church service, and the message of kingdom prosperity was on, by the man of God. I was listening, I prayed before leaving the church that day that God should show me more.

My beloved , this is what I know about kingdom secret, until YOU SEE IT, YOU DON'T HAVE IT, AND YOUR SEEING IT EMPOWERS YOUR UNDERSTANDING FAST, BECAUSE YOUR BLESSING DEPENDS ENTIRELLY ON YOUR UNDERSTANDING OF THE SUBJECT, IN THIS CASE WHICH IS TITHING.

Jesus perform two quick miracles as his last before leaving the earth,

1. **He opens their eyes**. (Luke:24v31).
2. **He opens their understanding**. (Luke:24v45).

I pray for you, that both your eyes and understanding be enlighten in the name of Jesus.

During the preaching, I heard the Holy Ghost, speak clearly to me in form of a question.

*" Have you ever seen anyone sowing and frowning their face?*

**No**, I answered. He said **why**?
Because they expect an harvest from the seed they sow"
Sept, 2016.

This was a higher level dimension to giving, meaning as you sew your seed in tithing and other giving. Be cheerful, expect to receive that which should give you Joy in your heart. *"God loves a cheerful giver".*
Also, this is an avenue to water your seed, why do I say so. If you frown to give, it means you are not giving willingly, you could as well take back the money, because there may not be reward or return.

So that attract Gods blessings to your giving, so water it with smiles, Joy in your heart. Thanks giving is the fruit of your lips and expectation as the hope in your heart. The Holy Spirit said, the reasons why people don't frown when giving, because they expect to receive back, and trust who they are giving to.
Another thing I will like to say here is that your giving progresses, with the knowledge of who God is. Let us get to know the Holy Spirit more through his word, and it will be easier for you to pay your tithe and give willingly.

*"Thus saith the Lord, let not the wise*

*man glory in his wisdom, Neither, let the mighty man glory in his might, let not the rich man Glory in his riches"*

*"But let him that glorieth glory in this, that he understandeth and knoweth me, that I am the LORD, which exercises loving Kindness, Judgement, and righteousness, in the earth for in these things I delight, saith the Lord."* ( Jere:9v23-24).

Some of you may be having little idea here, and a little principle, there about financial freedom, and accessing divine wealth, or you have not been able to plot or fix it together firmly, to become something you are sure of proven, tried and tested that works.

This knowledge by grace will give you that firmness of wisdom to give and receive in Jesus name. This grace to share has been on my heart since 2016, but I know that if I ever understand this truth and find the key I will share.

So the jack pot came to me suddenly, on March 30th, 2018, the Holy Spirit building on the previous truth. The light struck me from the message of a man of God I was listening to while at work. " The secret of financial prosperity, and I vow to grow and build on the light, until I became a practitioner with result. Mind you I have been paying my tithe, all this years, but having a totality of the knowledge and what to do, and how to do it to end in your own blessing is what is lacking in the Church today.

If not, what is now tithing?

**Every body tithes,** every body gives, at least once in a while, BUT WHY IS EVERY GIVER NOT BLESSED? WHY IS EVERY PASTOR NOT BLESSED AS A TITHER?

Answer to those question is, understanding the totality of the kingdom secret to finance and your approach to giving and sowing. This also includes WORKING HARD, to maintain inflow, of wealth.

*"The Lord shall open unto thee, his good treasure, The heaven to give thee rain unto thy land in his Season, and to bless all the works of thine hand, and thou shall lend unto many nation and thou shall not borrow"* Deut:28v12.

He said he himself will bless all the works of thine hand, meaning to become wealthy in the kingdom, one of the things you must do is to work. Do not keep your hands idle. So that God can have something to bless you with, I need a channel to send you my blessings. The same scripture applies here.

*" Seest thou a man diligent in his business, He shall stand before kings and not mean men"*

(Prov:22v29)

Your being diligent in business, in any area of your calling or field, will lift you up financially and otherwise, and when you work, you shall have enough to give and in reserve. Then you are blessed to be a blessing.

WHAT QUESTION DID THE HOLY SPIRIT ASK ME ON MARCH 30TH,2018.
THAT PROVOKE AND EVERLASTING ENCOUNTER TILL DATE.

" YOU DID NOT SOW, FROM WHERE DID YOU WANT TO REAP?" Holy Spirit.

That blessed evening, this wonderful word hit my heart hard. And I began searching more, I knew the Holy Spirit was set to do something new.

Few days later, I came to a FORMULAR that liberated me in my financial kingdom pursuit.

In this book, by grace I will attach the link to the march 10th video that sent the light, that provoked the formular for setting your finance right, and the video that answered the question of: You can sow, no matter what you earn.

From the second video, you will learn one great truth, which is,

IT IS YOUR MENTALITY OF HAVING AN EMPTY SAVING ACCOUNT THAT MAKES YOU THINK, ASSUME LACK AND EVERY TIME EXPECT TO BE BROKE SOON, BECAUSE THAT IS THE SIGNAL YOU RECEIVE.

But if you have savings, and you are a tither and a giver, When the spirit of lack and want come knocking with poverty thought.

Immediately, your sense, remind the spirit of lack that NO I AM NOT POOR. I have so much savings, this response happens in your thought within seconds and the spirit of lack goes away. Because you displayed Peace and confident. Why? Because you have money saved.

So it is welcoming the thought of lack that makes most of us embrace lack, and remain in want; because of lack of savings. This keep most people poor even while they tithe.

**It is planting a seed, and refuse to weed and water it. In the school of Kingdom finance, your SAVINGS IS WEEDING YOUR TITHE, and the words from your mouth after tithing is WATERING IT.**

You cannot received Gods blessings if after paying your tithe, the only thing you know how to say is: I don't think I can make it in this business or this ministry.

Please let your words align with the word of God upon your life.

*'You forgot that the expectation of the righteous shall Not be cut off" (Prov:23v18).*
*Secondly, that "You shall have whatsoever you say".*Mark:11v24

Learn how to save after tithing, learn how to maintain the right thought, control what you say from your mouth. Speak only what you want to see happen. And above all watch all your actions as you continue to water your seed. (Tithe), with diligence, diligence, and diligence.

Please let the direction and destination of your journey ( Calling), be seen and very visible from the way you work, this is called dedication.

May the Holy Spirit, empower you in Jesus name. Amen. As you take hold of this truth and more revealed to you by the Holy Spirit, you will see yourself sour to become a financial giant in the kingdom as a child of God in Jesus name.

By the inspiration of the Holy Spirit, I want to add

this, follow kingdom principles with instruction, with a pure heart to learn and apply.

*It is only in willingness and obedience will you eat the good of the land* **(the kingdom** (Isaiah:1v19). Let us dedicate ourselves in serving God obediently including in our finance, we will not miss our reward in Jesus name. Amen.

As I stood there on the platform, July 7th 2018, wondering how I can get large quantities of a book I just read on finance, and make it available to others, so that they too can be blessed.

Immediately, while I was still thinking, I heard the Holy Spirit spoke clearly to me, saying:

*" You write what you know and put the formula in there for them".*

so this is how this book was inspired and commanded to be written

Some one may ask, how come some unbelievers are rich in finance, and they don't serve God or Pay tithe, this similar question, was asked in the Bible by Gods people, and the Lord said, don't worry continue to obey me, and let me be the Judge, and you will see how the righteous shall be separated from the wicked at the end. (Mala:3v13-17).

Another person can say, what I earn is not enough; how can I give and pay my tithe. The link to the second video, attached to the book will explain that to you.

The truth is, no matter what you earn, as you decide to obey God, and follow instruction. You will see that, your little is enough, because it is only by giving, that we grow financially in the kingdom. May God enrich you abundantly.

# CHAPTER 5

## DIVINE FINANCIAL ANALYSIS.

## The income distribution FORMULAR.

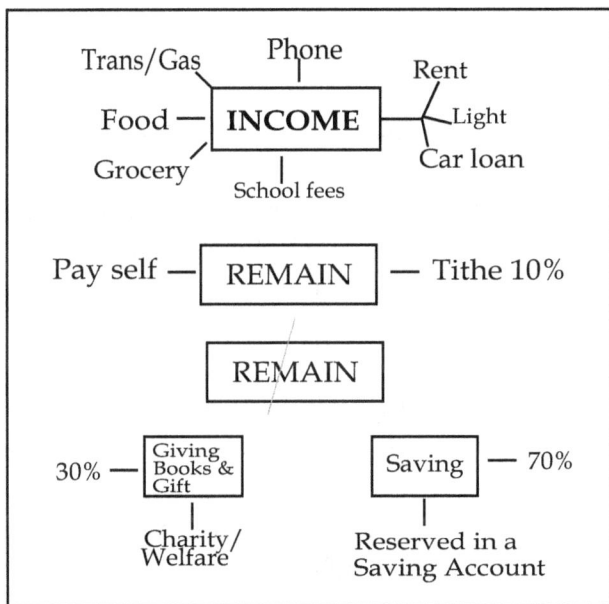

LINK VIDEO
*Bishop Oyedepo 2018: Secrets of Financial Empowerment*
*Pst Sam Adeyemi: Strategies action*

The above income distribution chat is almost self explanatory, please pay very close attention to this divinely inspired chat by the Holy Ghost.

If you look at the encounter above I had with the Holy Ghost, when he commanded this book;

*" You write your own, and put the formula in there for them"* The Holy Spirit.

So the chat above is the formula the Holy Spirit was referring to. So if not for this formula there will not be need for this book.  The main purpose of this book, was
To share my story and end it with this chat, which is able to establish you and help you master financial management until you are strong and it has become a part of you.

There is something I love and admire so much about this formula; it automatically teaches you how to save, ( if you have been finding it difficult to save from your income).  Even though the aim of the formula was to teach you tithing, you learn how to save, and simultaneously, open up for you a welfare account ; where you give out money easily, without touching your saving account.

My brethren, with this formula, no matter the amount of money in your pocket, or account, you will always have enough when this formula is obeyed.

This is what I and some of my students have been feeding from and enjoying the application of the divine secrets. This is not just telling you to tithe, but going further to reveal to you HOW TO! By practically applying your income through a given formula.

Anywhere in the world, where you find yourself, irrespective of your salary or income, just use the formula and you end up with, some money in your own personal account we call ( **SALARY**, because you pay yourself first), ( **WELFARE**…Money to give out)

( **SAVINGS**…Money set aside for huge projects or sudden occurrence ).

Now let me explain the chat from the beginning.
Let us assume, your income is $100. Or #100.

1.      First you begin by paying up all your BILLS.
**Example:** Rent, Car loan, School fees, Gas, Food, Phone bills, Groceries, Light and Water bill.

Lets assume you have $60 left after paying up all your bills.

2.      From the $60, take out %10 for TITHE; $6.

3.      Pay yourself as SALARY %10 another $6. (Pay your spouse, same $6 if you      a r e married and she is not working at t h e   t i m e ) . Balance $42.

4.      The next step is, you split the $42 into percentages of %30 and %70 percent respectively.

    Calculate %30 x$ in 42 =$12.6
    Calculate %70 x42  =$29.4.

5.      The next step is WELFARE: (Welfare account is what you give out to bless others, without welfare account, it is stressful to give people money, even your own family members). In this case, $12.6, will be in your welfare account.

So you do not touch your savings to give out money.
When you exhaust your welfare, wait till next month or paycheck, and go through the process

again.

6. The next step is your SAVINGS.
From the %70 of $42 we had, $29.4.
This will be in our savings account.
It is this money resting in your savings account that give you the grace, and wisdom to build wealth mentality and step into financial abundance in the kingdom.

PLEASE TAKE NOTE OF THIS,
**WHY MOST PEOPLE REMAIN POOR!**

Whenever you finish spending your salary, which is your second 10%.( Ten percent).
The spirit of poverty, will come knocking and attacking you with the spirit of fear, that you do not have enough money, that you are poor. If you have money saved in your savings account, your own spirit will fight back that evil thought immediately, taking your mind back to the money left in your savings, that you are **RICH.**

The thought of being rich continuously, on a daily basis, makes you end WEALTHY in the KINGDOM.

Continue this process, diligently with investment knowledge regarding your savings as revealed by the Holy Spirit, you will end up in abundant wealth.

# CHAPTER 6

## A BARRIER TO KINGDOM FINANCIAL PROSPERITY.

I just want to briefly highlight some misconception that most believers have about tithe and about giving in church.

1.     To make the Pastor rich.
To my understanding, you give to be blessed. If you understand, what your giving does to you and your family, as explained earlier, you won't hesitate to give.

Remember the Lord said, *I will build my church, and the gates of hell shall not prevail against it.*

*" And I say also unto thee, that thou art Peter, upon this rock I will build my Church, and the gates of hell shall not prevail against it."* Matt:16v18.

God is talking about standing against the devilish gates of hell, contending daily with the growth of his church. He has vowed to build it, including the life of the minister in all ramifications whatsoever. The Bible did not specify that if you do not give, the church will close down, or the pastor will come begging you for food. But that your giving is a result that you can be reached by Gods blessings. God loveth a cheerful giver, that I like so much. Whoever God loves he blesses.

God has a commitment to bless his servants that are faithful in his vineyard.

2.      The root of unbelief.

There is this understanding in most of us, that tithing isn't for us as Christians, some will say I can go to church and serve God, but not to pay my tithe or give money to church.

It was Bishop T.D Jakes that titled one of his messages, as **REPOSITION YOURSELF TO PROSPER!**

while are you standing in your own way of breakthrough with your unbelief in the word of God. Are you editing the Bible in what to obey and not obey.

It says: *if ye be willing and obedient, you shall eat the good of the land"* (Isaiah:1v19).

My beloved, you see, no one will come and force you, but will only encourage you to believe, so you can be blessed. GIVING IS RECEIVING those that don't give, don't receive.

I will say that even though we are Christians , some of us need to repent of our financial unbelief to prosper in the kingdom.
The Holy Spirit wants you to prosper. So a change of belief will open a new chapter for you in Jesus name. May God grant us understanding.

3.      A Word of Tithe in the New Testament.
Different   people have different contention, and various reason why they are not tithing.
Someone have ask me, show me a proof of tithing in the new testament and I will tithe.

By the help of the Holy Ghost, this scripture, which

was unknown to me before I was ask this question, was revealed to me by the Holy Ghost.

And behold, I gladly showed it to the brother, who was amazed to see, Jesus giving a command for tithing in the new testament. Please, my brethren, whatever your reasons are, it is not worth it. To enable you and I regain all that we may have lost and all the blessings that may be lying ahead for us in Christ Jesus.

*" And verily they that are of the sons of Levi, who receive the office of the priesthood, have a COMMANDMENT to take TITHE of the people, according to the Law of their brethren, though they come out of the loins of Abraham.*
(Heb:7v5).

Remain a blessing to this Generation in Jesus name. Amen.

# REVIEWED

As I stood there on the platform, wondering how I can get large quantities of a book I just read on finance, and make it available to others, so that they too can be blessed.

Immediately, while I was still thinking, I heard the Holy Spirit spoke clearly to me, saying:

" You write what you know and put the formula in there for them".

This book contains the financial formula for wealth management and growth in the kingdom. No matter who you are as a believer or where you live, you too can apply it and be blessed.

The author says that obeying Gods word and his voice, is an easy way out of every life challenges. Including financial struggle as some will like to call it.

 Ever since he realized through studies, that under Gods kingdom, there are rules for wealth. And certain principles must be obeyed, if we must taste of the good of the land.

This book will show you how to sow without stress.

# *FOOD FOR THOUGHT*

Money and Food are the same thing!
Infact they are partners.
Don't disrespect them,
Do not underestimate them,
And also don't ignore them.

Learn how to make, keep and PRESERVE them!
Because very soon in the next 15minutes you will
NEED them.

And if you don't have them it shows,
When you are hungry, you know and it Shows!
Also when you don't have money, you
acknowledge it and it shows too!

Then what should a man do to always have this
partners around?

**\*Make them your friend\***
By training and learning how to make and have
them around you, then one will know how to
preserve them.

Hmmm... Food and Money they are so humble, that
they don't have a Voice!
But others hear when they are speaking.
And lastly, remember they are to be shared in ideas,
wisdom and thought among friends.

#Take Baby Steps, But Keep Learning New Things
and Training!
*#Kingdom Wealth*
*Apostle Marvin*